Y

D0286753

YOUR WORD IS FIRE

The Hasidic Masters on Contemplative Prayer

edited and translated by

ARTHUR GREEN

and

BARRY W. HOLTZ

PAULIST PRESS
New York/Ramsey/Toronto

FRONTISPIECE ART

This illustration is from a "Mizrah" or prayer chart. Mizrah is the Hebrew word meaning "East." A "Mizrah" is a sign or decoration placed on the East wall of the home to remind those living there to face the East (Jerusalem) when they pray. This chart was created by an unknown Central European artist of the 19th Century who used the actual words of the Torah to create a design of the tablets by means of a process called microwriting.

Library of Congress
Catalog Card Number: 77-83589

ISBN: 0-8091-2047-X

Published by Paulist Press
Editorial Office: 1865 Broadway, New York, N.Y. 10023
Business Office: 545 Island Road, Ramsey, N.J. 07446

Printed and bound in the
United States of America

CONTENTS

For Kathy

who has taught us so much about these texts

and

to the memory of

Esther Schlosberg,

a woman of deep piety and devotion

who passed away

during the summer that

this book was created

INTRODUCTION

Judaism, we are told by the ancient rabbis, stands upon three pillars: Study of Torah, Worship, and the performance of Deeds of Love. The nature and relative importance of these three pillars of religious life, the intellectual, the devotional, and the activist, have been debated by rabbis and their disciples over the course of many centuries. It was always assumed that the three were deeply intertwined, and that a proper balance among them formed the ideal of Jewish religiosity. No one of these three values was ever allowed to totally supplant the others; nevertheless, there were times and places in the history of Judaism in which one value or another seemed to achieve the place of primacy in the minds of pious reflecting Jews.

This is nowhere as clear as in the early period of Hasidism, that great movement of religious revival that brought new spirit to the lives of Jews in the towns and villages of Poland and the Ukraine toward the latter half of the eighteenth century. Here worship, particularly in the form of contemplative prayer, came to be clearly identified as the central focus of the Jew's religious life. Both the ecstatic outpourings of ordinary people and the highly sophisticated treatments of devotional psychology in the works of the Hasidic masters bear witness to this new and unique emphasis upon the inner life of prayer.

Hasidism views all of Jewish life as "the way of

service." Man's only task in life is the service of God; prayer, study, and all of the commandments are seen instrumentally: they are the means by which the Jew may fulfill his sacred task. Thus the rabbinic ideal of "study for its own sake" has to be scrutinized and reinterpreted as study for the sake of God, a conscious act of service. Hasidic authors tirelessly warn their readers against the dangers of robot-like performance of the commandments. Each ritual act must have its way lighted by the glow of inner devotion, else it "has no wings" and cannot ascend to God. Even acts of human kindness, the "Deeds of Love" of which the rabbis had spoken, are here seen in devotional terms: there is no higher sacred act than that of helping another to discover the presence of God within his own soul.

The core of "service" as seen in Hasidism is the fulfillment of that desire, deeply implanted within each human soul, to return to its original state of oneness with God. Prayer, by its very nature pointing to the intimate relationship between God and soul, becomes the focal point of Hasidic religiosity. The Ba'al Shem Tov (1700-1760), the first great master of the movement, was told by heaven that all his spiritual attainments derived not from any claim to scholarship (as was commonly to be expected in non-Hasidic circles of the time), but rather from the great devotion with which he prayed.

The ecstatic quality of prayer-life in early Hasidism has been described in many ways. The Ba'al Shem Tov was said to tremble so greatly in his prayer that bits of grain in a nearby barrel were seen to join him in his trembling. A disciple who touched the master's prayer-garment was so seized with tremors that he had to pray for release. One of the followers was so overcome by ecstasy while preparing for prayer in the ritual bath that he ran from the bathhouse to the adjoining synagogue and danced on the tables without realizing he was not fully dressed. Strange and seemingly inhuman noises, violent movements of the body, even the turning of cartwheels before the Torah, all characterized the devotional climate of some early Hasidic groups. The masters themselves sometimes felt called upon to restore the values of inwardness and silence to a world where unbridled mystical ecstasy was coming to be the order of the day.

What was it about, all this ecstatic frenzy? Prayer was surely not a new discovery for the Jew in the eighteenth century. For nearly two thousand years pious Jews had been reciting their daily liturgy, morning, afternoon, and evening. It had been said of the second-century Rabbi Akiva that if you left him praying in one corner of a room, you were sure to return to find him in the opposite corner, so enthusiastic was his style of worship. Medieval mystics in Germany, France, and Spain had devoted much of their attention to the secrets of inward prayer, turning the recitation of the obligatory liturgy into a setting for the ascent of the soul into ever-higher realms of spiritual existence. Why then all the commotion about prayer at this late date, to the point where the great rabbis of the day were confused and frightened by the forms worship took in the emerging movement?

In order to understand this renewed excitement over prayer, we must realize that Hasidism was, in the truest sense, a *revival* movement, one that seeks to bring new life to old forms that are ever faced with the dangers of petrification and decay. The strength of Judaism has always been its ability to at once preserve and renew its most ancient forms. This is especially true with regard to liturgical prayer. The power of liturgy lies largely in its sameness and constant repetition, but in that same familiarity lies the potential downfall of such prayer as it degenerates into mere mechanistic recitation. The Ba'al Shem Tov and his followers were acutely aware of this problem. They knew that prayer could only work if it were a constant source for the rediscovery of God's immanent presence in the world.

The mystical ecstasy of Hasidism flows from the rediscovery that God is present in all of human life. All things and all moments are vessels that contain the Presence. "The whole earth is filled with His glory!" The old Kabbalistic formula "There is no place devoid of Him" became an ecstatic outcry in early Hasidism. Since all of Creation is filled with God's Presence, there is neither place nor moment that cannot become an opening in which one may encounter Him. Hasidism thus teaches that all of life is an extension of the hour of prayer, and that prayer itself is the focal point around which one's entire day is centered.

The followers of the Ba'al Shem Tov were not the first to assert the primacy of prayer in Judaism. For two hundred years before the birth of Hasidism, the mystic teachers who followed in the path of R. Isaac Luria (1534-1572) of Safed had already placed boundless store in the power of man to uplift the fallen worlds by means of meditative prayer.

Luriannic prayer was filled with a kind of urgent and theurgic messianism: by means of an infinitely complex system of theosophical meditations, in which each word and letter of prayer was used to address a particular configuration of the divine potencies, man could bring about the long-awaited redemption of Israel and the world.

Hasidism continued in the Luriannic path, but with two important changes. From the outset, Hasidic piety contained within it an ideal of simplicity. Hasidism may indeed be viewed socially as both the political and spiritual self-assertion of the poorly educated lower classes against the elitism of the abstrusely learned. Thus the complex contemplative system of the Luriannic Kabbalists, which itself required a great deal of esoteric learning, became intolerable as an ideal. The word spoken with simple wholeness of heart came to be more highly valued than that spoken with deep knowledge of esoteric symbols: the depths of contemplation became open to all who sought truly to enter them. One of the masters explained this change in values by the parable of the keys and the lock. In former times, the mystics had access to a complicated series of keys that could unlock the heart in prayer. We no longer have the keys; all we can do is to smash the lock. The only true prerequisite for such prayer, he said, is a broken heart.

The nature of the redemption to be brought about by prayer was also transformed in Hasidism. Largely because of the tragic failure of messianism in the Sabbatian uprising, the use of prayer as a direct vehicle for historic redemption was underplayed in Hasidic teachings. By means of *devequt*, or intimate attachment to God, one could come to personally transcend all the trials of life in the world, while the external historical situation in fact remained unchanged. Redemption *within* this world became the goal. For some Hasidic authors, the *devequt* state as attained by the individual came to replace *tiqqun*, eschatological world-redemption, as the central goal of the religious life.

II

The revolution contained in the Hasidic attitude toward liturgical prayer was perhaps best expressed by R. Pinhas of Korzec. "People think," he said, "that they pray *to* God. But this is not the case. For prayer itself *is* of the very essence of God!"

Prayer is God! The statement seems, at first reading, to be a simple outpouring of ecstasy, the particular meaning of which is difficult to determine. But in fact such a statement is a radical formulation of deeply rooted Hasidic ideas, which form the background of the movement's fascination with prayer.

The human soul, according to Hasidic teachings, is "a part of God above." Religious devotion is caused by the longing of the soul to be reunited with its source, from which it has been separated in the process of human individuation. While souls differ from one another in their inner nature according to their various "roots" of origin above, and while each soul must find its own individual path to *devequt*, all souls can come together in the outpouring process of prayer. Prayer, and particularly when employing the Hebrew liturgical text, is the vehicle through which the spark of God within the soul may come face to face with the God beyond it. Thus prayer itself *is* the process of *yihud*, the unification of God, always proclaimed by the Kabbalists to be the highest goal of life.

This glorification of the text of prayer is further rooted in the fascination with the mystery of the word, which has always characterized Jewish spirituality. The Biblical account of Creation, in which God creates the world by the mysterious power of speech, plays a formative role in all of later Jewish piety. Augmented by the Kabbalistic creation myth, in which God is said to create through the permutations of chains of Hebrew letters, it sets the mysticism of words and letters as one of the central themes of Jewish religious literature. Liturgical prayer recited in the holy tongue, say the Hasidic masters, is but a reordering of the letters through which God created and revealed his Torah. Man takes those same letters, forms them into the words of prayer, and brings them back to God. Thus soul and word are undergoing the same process in prayer: they help to carry one another in their shared journey of return to their source in God. In order to pray deeply, a man must truly enter into the letters, until he sees the light of God's Creation, which still dwells within them.

The centrality of word and letter mysticism in Hasidic thinking is perhaps best illustrated by a well-known story, various versions of which are often quoted in the name of the Hasidic masters. There was once a simple man who used to address God in prayer and say: "Lord of the World! You know that I have not studied, that I cannot even read the holy words of Your prayer-book. All I remember of that which I learned as a child is the alphabet itself. But surely You, Lord, know all the words. So I will give you the letters of the alphabet, and You can form the words Yourself." And so he prayed, reciting the letters of the alphabet: "*Aleph, Bet, Gimel . . .* "

The story, like many Hasidic tales, is not so simple as it first appears. Here two of the great ideals of Hasidic devotion have been combined: the virtue of simplicity and the fascination with the creative powers of the letters, the building-blocks of both divine and human speech. The divine energy of Creation formed the universe through the power of the word; God's speech, in fact, like that of man, may be made accessible if reduced to the constituent letters of the alphabet. In the tale, the simple man has nothing to offer the Lord but the letters. Yet the same is true of the most sophisticated contemplative among the masters. All of us are "simple"; all that we can do in prayer is to return the letters of Creation to their source above.

III

The masters of Hasidic prayer, like most of their predecessors in the Jewish mystical tradition, were hesitant to write down any sort of systematic guide to the ways of contemplation. While they did have a clear sense (particularly in the school of the Maggid of Miedzyrzec) that there were specific ordered steps to be taken that could lead one up the devotional ladder, the composition of such a guide would have been a particular affront to their ideals of spontaneity and wholeness. By what steps in a manual can you guide a man to *hitlahavut*, that state where ecstasy fills his heart like a burning fire? Can any studied method really lead one to know that his own soul is nothing but an outpouring of God's light?

Yet despite this lack of systematic introduction, the works of the early Hasidic masters are filled with hints as to the various rungs of inner prayer and how they are to be attained. From these references, scattered throughout early Hasidic literature, a composite picture of their approach to contemplative prayer can be reconstructed. It should be emphasized, however, that the following attempt at systematization is not directly to be found in any single Hasidic source, but is rather culled from the advice of various masters in various situations of spiritual guidance.

There are two types of prayer-state generally described in Hasidic sources. *Qatnut*, the "lower" or ordinary state in which one generally begins his prayers, is opposed to *gadlut*, the "greater" or expanded state of mystical consciousness. Prayer recited while in a state of *qatnut* may contain within it great devotion; it is generally the simple prayer devotion of giving oneself to God and accepting His will. It may contain both the love of God and man's awe before His Presence, the two essential qualities for authentic prayer in Hasidism. In *qatnut*, however, man is not transported beyond himself; he does not "ascend" to a world where consciousness is transformed or where self-awareness is transcended.

The ascent from this state to that of *gadlut* is one

of the central themes of Hasidic prayer literature. While the simple devotions of the *qatnut* state are highly valued, the true goal of the worshiper is to enter that world where "he may come to transcend time," where "distinctions between 'life' and 'death', 'land' and 'sea', have lost their meaning." He seeks to "concentrate so fully on his prayer that he no longer is aware of his own self . . . to step outside the body's limits." Rapturous descriptions of the state of *gadlut* abound in Hasidic writings.

The first step in the attainment of *gadlut* is the involvement of the entire self in the act of worship. There must be no reservation, no holding back of a part of the person. The body is to be involved along with the soul in the act of prayer: the rhythmic movement of the body, the sometimes loud outcry of the voice, the training of the eye to the page—all these externals are aids, in the first stages of prayer, to the involvement of the entire self.

As the ecstatic power of this involvement begins to overwhelm him, the worshiper may begin to dispense with the externals, one by one, as he feels ready to do so. His body may become still, his shout may become a whisper, and he may put the book aside and see the letters of his prayer with the mind's eye alone.

At this point, the winged ascent of soul and word to the upper worlds begins in earnest. Prayer must ever be accompanied by the love and fear of God, the two emotions Jewish teachers had long seen as the "wings" that allow one's prayer to ascend to God. Each moment of true prayer contains within it the moment of standing before the Lord at Sinai, when the consuming love of God and the total awe before His tremendous power were most fully combined. As love and fear accompany the word upward, the letters become liberated from their verbal patterns, and lead the soul back from the "World of Speech" to their higher source in the "World of Thought." Verbal prayer gives way to abstract contemplation, to a liberation of the worshiper's mind from all content other than his attachment to God. First all of one's energies are concentrated on the word as spoken with fulness; now the word itself is released, and nothing remains with the worshiper but the fulness of heart that, paradoxically, also marks him as an empty vessel, ready to receive the light from above. Even the self-conscious feeling of this fulness must be transcended, for "a person who still knows how intensely he is praying has not yet overcome his awareness of self."

This description of the ascent from the verbal to the wholly contemplative state parallels the structure of the cosmos as it had been depicted by the earlier Jewish esoteric tradition. The "World of Speech" is here identified with the *shekhinah* (translated throughout this work as "Presence"), the lowest of the ten divine manifestations around which the speculative content of that tradition had centered. *Shekhinah* is the Presence of God in the lower world, the indwelling glory of God that fills all of Creation. It is generally depicted by the mystics in feminine terms; the divinity that inhabits both world and soul longs to be reunited with her transcendent spouse. The "World of Thought" mentioned in these sources refers to *Ḥokhmah* ("Wisdom," "Sophia") the highest of the ten rungs according to Hasidic reckoning. The movement of the worshiper from speech to abstract thought is thus often depicted as a journey of ascent through the realms of divine light.

This emptying of the mind of all content, which Hasidic prayer shares with many other meditative techniques, finally leads man to that place within God known as the "Nothing" or the realm of Primordial Nothingness. According to Kabbalistic theology, this Nothingness *within* God is the *ayin* or *nihil* out of which the world was created. All things are rooted in the divine "No-thing." As prayer ascends to God, the creative energy is returned to its predefined source in the One. Creation, however, is viewed in Hasidism as a constant ongoing process: the world is ever pouring forth anew from this state of Nothingness, which lies at the innermost core of divinity. As the worshiper's mind is emptied, he stands ready to be filled once again, having returned to that source from which Creation takes place.

Here one has reached the moment of ultimate transformation. In all change and growth, say the masters, the mysterious *ayin* is present. There is an ungraspable instant in the midst of all transformation when that which is about to be transformed is no longer that which it had been until that moment, but has not yet emerged as its transformed self; that moment belongs to the *ayin* within God. Since change and transformation are *constant*, however, in fact all moments are moments of contact with the *ayin*, a contact that man is usually too blind to acknowledge. The height of contemplative prayer is seen as such a transforming moment, but one that is marked by awareness. The worshiper is no longer himself, for he is fully absorbed, in that moment, in the Nothingness of divinity. In that moment of absorption the worshiper is transformed: as he continues his verbal prayer, it is no longer he who speaks, but rather the Presence who speaks through him. In that prayerful return to the source the human being has reached his highest state, becoming nought but the passive instrument for the ever self-proclaiming praise of God. Through his lips the divine word is spoken.

IV

Any teaching that places such great emphasis on total concentration in prayer must of course deal with the question of distraction. What is a person to do when "alien thoughts" enter his mind and lead him away from prayer? Sometimes it seems that the more intensely one tries to concentrate, the more powerful and even sinful those thoughts become. How is one to be saved from seeing his prayer become a battlefield in which distraction and self-castigation alternate to keep him far from God? Surely one who is busily punishing himself for the evil of his wayward thoughts cannot have the joy and wholeness that are needed for His service.

It is perhaps in response to this problem that the Ba'al Shem Tov's thought was most revolutionary. He spoke against the attempts of his contemporaries to either do battle with distracting thoughts or to see them as vanities that should simply be ignored. Just as in life he taught that each moment may be an opening to the Presence of God, so in prayer he taught that each distraction may become a ladder by

which one may ascend to a new level of devotion.
For if one truly believes that all things are from God
and bear His mark, he can make no exception for
the fantasies of his own mind! They too are from
God, and are sent to us as ways to His service. The
worshiper must break open the shell of evil
surrounding the distracting thought, find the root of
that thought in God, and join it to his prayer. Thus if
a person is distracted by sexual desire during his
worship, he should not seek to drive that desire from
his mind, but rather should come to know that such
desire itself is but a fallen spark from the World of
Love, which seeks to be uplifted in the ascent of his
prayer. When the Talmud states that a prayer leader
who repeats his words and says: "Hear, hear, O
Israel!" is to be silenced (probably for fear of
dualistic heresy), the Ba'al Shem Tov comments:
Why should the poor man be silenced? Perhaps
when he said the first "Hear" he was distracted by
some other thought, and repeated the word only to
pray more devoutly! But that is the very root of
dualism! In repeating the word, he is denying the
legitimacy of his former prayer; he is denying that
God was present in that moment of distraction! And
only he who truly knows that God is present in *all*
things, including those thoughts he seeks to flee, can
be a leader of prayer.

Behind this matter lies the Ba'al Shem Tov's
all-pervading commitment to the full integration of
the self, a commitment that was not shared by all of
his disciples. The founder of Hasidism deeply
believed that a man torn by inner struggles was not
yet ready to come to God. Hence his comments
denouncing excessive worry about minor sins.
Brooding on one's sinfulness, he taught, was merely

a trick by the Evil One to keep man far from God. The service of God requires the deepest joy, and such joy cannot be experienced in a divided self. Repent of evil, know that God in His love accepts your penitence, and return to serve Him with joy and wholeness.

V

Because Hasidic literature contains no systematic manual of contemplative prayer, the texts included in the present volume have been culled from many sources. A large number of them have been previously collected in such Hebrew anthologies as *Sefer Ba'al Shem Tov*, by Simeon Mendel Vednik of Gavartchov; *Romemut Ha-Tefillah,* by Shelomo Rosenthal of Warsaw; and *Derekh Hasidim* by Nahman of Cheryn. In all cases, however, the translators have referred to the original sources of the material, as indicated in the notes to this volume.

While the notes may be of some interest to students of Hasidism, the primary purpose of the present translation is devotional rather than academic. We offer these texts for the enrichment of the personal religious lives of our readers, for use as readings in the context of worship, and as a source of inspiration to those who seek to uncover the oneness of religious truth behind the garb of various mystical traditions. It is our belief that the authentic voice of Hasidic devotion, properly presented for the contemporary reader, may still speak to our spiritual situation.

The translations in this volume are the product of careful and, we hope successfully so, meticulous work. We have taken pains not to reinterpret, but rather to allow the Hasidic masters to speak for themselves. It should be noted, however, that the complete lack of concern for literary style on the part of the Hasidic authors did necessitate some rearrangement and condensing of material. Hasidic homiletic texts, in which the prayer instruction literature is often to be found, are repetitive and sometimes garbled notes in Hebrew for longer sermons that were preached in Yiddish. As such, they at times require some structural rewording when presented in translation, which necessarily involves an attempt to return them, in the translator's mind, to their original language and context.

The sources of this collection are the teachings of the Ba'al Shem Tov, the Maggid Dov Baer of Miedzyrzec, and their immediate disciples, in the latter part of the eighteenth century. Works of such particular Hasidic schools as Lubavitch and Bratslav, which differ quite radically both in style and content from these teachings, have not been included.

It should be emphasized that the texts found in this volume did not originate in abstract thought. Many were undoubtedly said to disciples who came to their masters with particular problems in their prayer-lives. Similarly, this translation is intended for use: it is our hope that this offering will contribute significantly to the rebirth of serious religious life as nurtured by the sources of Judaism.

THE POWER
OF
YOUR PRAYER

What a great wonder that man should be able to
    draw so near to God in prayer.
How many walls there are between man and God!
Even though God fills all the world,
    He is so very hidden!
Yet a single word of prayer can topple all the walls
    and bring you close to God.

When a Jew speaks a word of prayer
  in love and awe,
  the power of his word gives birth
  to God's glory.
The angels call out to God:
  "Who is like Your Israel,
  a unique people in the world!"
How great is even a single word of such prayer:
  it causes all the angels to sing to God!
All the worlds join with man as he serves his Lord.

This is the meaning of "The Song of Songs"—
  one who sings a song below can
  arouse many songs on high!

Once a wise man was asked: "On what thought do
    you concentrate as you pray?"
He replied: "I bind myself to the Divine Life
    that flows through all of God's creations.
    As I join myself to each
    I seek to bring the life within it back to God."
"Destroyer!" said the other. "How can the world
    exist if you draw out all its life?"
The wise man remained unperturbed:
    "Do you really think I can do all that—
    I who have so little power?"
"But in that case," replied the other,
    "of what value is your prayer?"

The truth is that you must believe
    in the power of your prayer.
The truly wise, who stand before the King in prayer,
    surely can bind themselves to the flow of Life.
But they are not allowed to do so always—
    lest by their uplifting powers
    they do indeed destroy the world.

It is possible to be so humble
      that your very humility
      keeps you far from God.
A humble person may not believe that his own
      prayer
      can cause the Presence
      to flow through all the worlds.
But how then can you believe
      that even angels are nourished
      by your words?

Know the power of your prayer
      and serve your God in fullness!

Why do the prayers of the righteous at times
       seem to go unanswered?

There is a king who has two sons.
Each of them comes to receive his gift
       from the royal table.
The first son appears at his father's doorway,
       and as soon as he is seen, his request is granted.
The father holds this son in low esteem,
       and is annoyed by his presence.
The king orders that the gifts be handed
       to his son at the door
       so that he will not approach the table.

Then the king's
       beloved son appears.
The father takes great pleasure in this son's arrival
       and does not want him to leave too quickly.
For this reason the king delays granting his request,
       hoping that the son will then draw near to him.
As the son comes closer,
       he feels his father's love so deeply
       that he does not hesitate to stretch forth
       his own hand to the royal table.

Both of the sons receive
       what they had sought from their father;
       the portions in themselves are no different.
But the first son receives his gifts in shame,
       seeing that his father stays so far from him.
His brother, however, has come so close to the king
       that he himself can take that which he needs.

Of communal prayer it has been told:

Once in a tropical country, a certain splendid bird,
more colorful than any that had ever been seen,
was sighted at the top of the tallest tree.
The bird's plumage contained within it
all the colors in the world.
But the bird was perched so high
that no single person
could ever hope to reach it.

When news of the bird reached the ears of the king,
he ordered that a number of men
try to bring the bird to him.
They were to stand on one another's shoulders
until the highest man could reach the bird
and bring it to the king.
The men assembled near the tree,
but while they were standing
balanced on one another's shoulders,
some of those near the bottom
decided to wander off.
As soon as the first man moved,
the entire chain collapsed,
injuring several of the men.
Still the bird remained uncaptured.

The men had doubly failed the king.
For even greater than his desire to see the bird
was his wish to see his people
so closely joined to one another.

PREPARING
THE
WAY

Faith is the basis of all worship;
    only the truly faithful can pray each day.
And what is the basis of faith?
    "He renews each day the work of Creation."
The faithful one sees
    that every day is a new Creation,
    that all the worlds are new,
    that he himself has just been born.
How could he not want to sing
    the praise of his Creator?

If he does not have the faith
    that God creates anew each day,
    prayer becomes an old, unwanted habit.
How difficult it is to say
    the same words day after day!
Thus scripture says: "Cast us not into old age!"—
    may the word never become old for us.

Take special care to guard your tongue
    before the morning prayer.
Even greeting your fellowman, we are told,
    can be harmful at that hour.
A person who wakes up in the morning is
    like a new creation.
Begin your day with unkind words,
    or even trivial matters—
        even though you may later turn to prayer,
    you have not been true to your Creation.
All of your words each day
    are related to one another.
All of them are rooted
    in the first words that you speak.

No matter what the season,
   one should take special care
   to begin his prayer before sunrise.
Most of the service should be completed
   before the sun appears.
The great difference between prayer at dawn
   and prayer recited later in the day
   can hardly be imagined.
Before dawn one can still combat
   the destructive forces of the coming day.
But once the sun is out upon the earth,
   "nothing is hidden from its heat."
Do not consider this a small thing,
   for the Master himself
   took such great care in this matter
   that he would even worship without a quorum
   in order to say his prayers at the proper hour.

A person of spirit may begin his prayer
    in awe and trembling,
    saying to himself:
    "Who am I, a poor clod of earth,
    to stand before the King of Kings in prayer?"

He speaks only a partial truth.
He does not yet know the higher truth, however—
    the truth that all things,
    even the material world,
    are filled with God's presence.
Indeed he cannot speak the words of prayer—
    better that he remain silent before the Lord.

Thus scripture says:
    "God is in heaven and you are upon the earth;
    do not rush to speak, and let your words be
    few."
As long as you believe that God is only in heaven
    and does not fill the earth—
    let your words be few.
Only when you come to know
    that you too contain His Presence—
    only then can you begin to pray.

How much more pleasing to God is prayer in joy
    than that which is said in sadness and tears!

A poor man begs and weeps
    as he comes before the king;
    he can be dismissed with but a trifle.
But when a noble prince steps forward,
    the king's praises joyfully on his lips,
    and then asks some favor,
    he cannot be treated so lightly.
To him the king grants his greatest gifts—
    a prince must receive a princely portion.

Before you begin to pray,
    decide that you are ready to die
    in that very prayer.
There are some people so intense in their worship,
    who give up so much of their strength to prayer,
    that if not for a miracle they would die
    after uttering only two or three words.
It is only through God's great kindness
    that such people live,
    that their soul does not leave them
    as they are joined to Him in prayer.

There are times when you must prepare yourself
    before you can pray.
Reciting Psalms or studying Torah before prayer
    may provide the strength you need.
But take care also to avoid giving yourself too fully
    to these preparations,
    lest they consume all your strength
    and leave no room for prayer itself.

Enter into prayer slowly.
Do not exhaust your strength,
    but proceed step by step.
Even if you are not aroused as your prayer begins,
    give close attention to the words you speak.
As you grow in strength
    and God helps you to draw near,
    you can even say the words more quickly
    and remain in His Presence.

The evil urge has two ways
    of keeping you from prayer;
To each there is an appropriate response.

At times its voice will say to you:
    "Who are you, son of man,
    that you dare come into this holy place
    to speak before the Lord?
    How dare you pray—you man of unclean lips,
    you who are so filled with sin!"
If you hear these words, reply:
    "See all the good I have done!
    See the way I have kept the Lord's
    commandments,
    how much joy I have brought Him with my
    prayer!"

But even your reply can become an opening
    for the voice of evil.
For the evil urge can also dress itself
    in pride and say:
    "You are the leader of all Israel,
    the greatest of all!
    Surely humility is no virtue
    for one so great as you.
    What a great scholar you are!
    How carefully you fulfill God's commands!"
Know then that this too is the trap
    of the evil one and say:
    "How great are my sins! How empty my
    devotion!
    I have not fulfilled
    even a single one of God's commands!"

There are many people who turn
    the words of prayer into songs.
They even go so far as to plan out
    their worship, saying:
    "Here I will sing this melody; there, another."
They call this the service of God and hope to reach
    states of ecstasy by such song.
They even believe
    that God is pleased by such worship!
What fools they are—
    they walk in darkness
    and have not seen the truth.

A person who is truly at prayer
    must seek to go beyond the material world.
He should speak the words simply,
    and devote all his attention
    to the holy letters
    and to the meaning of his prayer.
It is this true devotion
    that will bring him to the love and fear of God—
    and will really set his heart aflame.

MEET HIM
IN THE
WORD

"Make yourself an ark of gopher wood
. . . make a window for the ark
and finish it to a cubit above;
and set the door of the ark in its side;
make it with lower, second and third decks.
. . . Go into the ark,
you and all your household. . . . "

The ark of Noah is the word of prayer.
"Make yourself a window for the ark":
Let the words of prayer
be a window through which
you see to the ends of the earth.

The window is the "light" in the ark
which is the word: Speak the word
in such a way
that the inner light shines through it.

"Make it with lower, second, and third decks."
Each letter contains worlds and souls
and the Presence of God.
As the letters are joined to one another
and form the words of prayer,
all that is within them
rises up to God.
He who joins his soul
to this process
brings all the worlds together in boundless joy.

"Go into the ark,
you and all your household"
—enter into the word
with all your body,
with all your strength.

How does a person come to know God's hidden
    ways?

The stars, which by day are not visible,
    can nevertheless be seen
    by one who uses a proper lens.
The holy letters of prayer form such lenses;
    they may be used as telescopes for seeing into
    the hidden ways of God.
One who has already transcended his own self
    and has come to know
    that he is nothing—
    such a person can look so deeply
    into the letters
    that the divine qualities of which they speak
    become real to him.
As he says "the great" in his prayer,
    the greatness of God comes to him
    in those very letters.
Thus he sees the power of God
    in the words "the powerful,"
    the awe of God in the words "the awesome."
The letters themselves have the power
    to draw forth these qualities from above.

It is through the letters
    that the word of God
    may come to dwell with man.

Think that the letters of prayer
    are the garments of God.
What a joy to be making a garment
    for the greatest of kings!
Enter into every letter with all your strength.
God dwells within each letter;
    as you enter it, you become one with Him.

See your prayer as arousing the letters
  through which heaven and earth
  and all living things were created.
The letters are the life of all;
  when you pray through them,
  all Creation joins with you in prayer.
All that is around you can be uplifted;
  even the song of a passing bird
  may enter into such a prayer.

A person should put all his strength into the words,
    proceeding from letter to letter
    with such concentration
    that he loses awareness of his bodily self.
It then seems to him that the letters themselves
    are flowing into one another.
This uniting of the letters is his greatest joy.
If joy is felt as two human bodies come together,
    how much greater must be the joy
    of this union in spirit!

Know that each word of prayer is a complete self.
If all of your strength is not in it,
    it is born incomplete,
    like one lacking a limb.

When you focus all your thought
        on the power of the words,
        you may begin to see the sparks of light
        that shine within them.
The sacred letters are the chambers
        into which God pours His flowing light.
The lights within each letter, as they touch,
        ignite one another,
        and new lights are born.

It is of this the Psalmist says:
        "Light is sown for the righteous,
        and joy for the upright in heart."

"With the Lord your God"

God is present in the words of Torah.
Enter into the words,
    speaking them with all your strength.
Your soul will then meet God in the word—
    that soul which is itself a part of God above.

This is the true union of the Holy One, blessed be
    He,
    and His Presence, of which the mystics speak.
"With the Lord your God"—with the Lord, *your*
    God—
    the Presence within you, *your* God,
    is joined together with "the Lord"—
    its eternal source.

If prayer is pure and untainted,
    surely that holy breath
    that rises from your lips
    will join with the breath of heaven
    that is always flowing
    into you from above.
Thus our masters have taught the verse
    "Every breath shall praise Him":
    with every single breath that you breathe,
    He is praised.
As the breath leaves you, it ascends to God,
    and then it returns to you from above.
Thus that part of God
    which is within you
    is reunited with its source.

The purpose of all prayer is to uplift the words,
 to return them to their source above.
The world was created
 by the downward flow of letters:
The task of man is to form those letters into words
 and take them back to God.
If you come to know this dual process,
 your prayer may be joined
 to the constant flow of Creation—
 word to word, voice to voice,
 breath to breath, thought to thought.

The words fly upward and come before Him.
As God turns to look at the ascending word,
 life flows through all the worlds
 and prayer receives its answer.
All this happens in an instant
 and all this happens continually;
Time has no meaning in the sight of God.
The divine spring is ever-flowing;
 one who is ready can make himself into a
 channel
 to receive the waters from above.

When a person prays in an ordinary way,
    the words of prayer have no life of their own.
It is only the name of God appearing in their midst
    that gives them life.
Thus when you recite the words:
    "Blessed art Thou, O Lord . . . , "
    life does not enter the words
    until the word "Lord" is uttered.

But when a true master of prayer recites the words
    every word is a name of God.
"Blessed" is a name, "Thou" is a name. . . .

Do not think that the words of prayer
    as you say them
    go up to God.
It is not the words themselves that ascend;
    it is rather the burning desire of your heart
    that rises like smoke toward heaven.
If your prayer consists only of words and letters,
    and does not contain your heart's desire—
    how can it rise up to God?

BEYOND
THE WALLS
OF SELF

"Go out of the ark,
  you and your wife and your children."

Take *yourself* out of the words of your prayer.
Let your prayer not be for yourself
  or for your household,
    but only for the sake of God and His Presence.

A person should be so absorbed in prayer
        that he is no longer
        aware of his own self.
There is nothing for him but the flow of Life;
        all his thoughts are with God.
He who still knows how intensely he is praying
        has not yet overcome the bonds of self.

You must forget yourself in prayer.
Think of yourself as nothing
    and pray only for the sake of God.
In such prayer you may come to transcend time,
    entering the highest realms
    of the World of Thought.
There all things are as one;
Distinctions between "life" and "death,"
    "land" and "sea,"
    have lost their meaning.
But none of this can happen
    as long as you remain attached
    to the reality of the material world.
Here you are bound to the distinctions
    between good and evil
    that emerge only in the lower realms of God.
How can one who remains attached to his own self
    go beyond time to the world where all is one?

The human body is always finite;
It is the spirit that is boundless.
Before he begins to pray,
    a person should cast aside that which limits him
    and enter the endless world of Nothing.
In prayer he should turn to God alone
    and have no thoughts of himself at all.
Nothing but God exists for him;
    he himself has ceased to be.
The true redemption of man's soul can only happen
    as he steps outside the body's limits.

In prayer seek to make yourself into a vessel
    for God's Presence.
God, however, is without limit;
"Endless" is His name.
How can any finite vessel hope to contain
    the endless God?
Therefore, see yourself as nothing:
    only one who is nothing
    can contain the fulness
    of the Presence.

As long as you can still say the words
    "Blessed art Thou"
    by your own will,
      know that you have not yet reached
      the deeper levels of prayer.
Be so stripped of selfhood that you have
    neither the awareness
    nor the power
      to say a single word on your own.

Why are we told to recite the verse
    "O Lord, open my lips
    and let my mouth declare Your praise"
    before our most sacred prayer?
Like banks to a river,
    lips form the outer edges of human speech.
We pray that God may release us from those limits,
    so that our mouths may declare
    His endless praise.

As a person begins his prayer, reciting the words:
    "O Lord, open my lips
    and let my mouth declare Your praise,"
    the Presence of God comes into him.
Then it is the Presence herself
    who commands his voice;
    it is she who speaks the words *through* him.
One who knows in faith
    that all this happens within him
    will be overcome with trembling
    and with awe.

There are times when the love of God
   burns so powerfully within your heart
   that the words of prayer seem to rush forth,
   quickly and without deliberation.
At such times it is not you yourself who speak;
   rather it is *through* you
   that the words are spoken.

When you speak, think that the World of Speech is
    at work within you,
    for without that presence,
    you would not be able to speak at all.
Similarly, you would not think at all were it not
    for the World of Thought within you.
Man is like a ram's horn;
    the only sound he makes is
    that which is blown through him.
Were there no one blowing into the horn,
    there would be no sound at all.

There are two rungs of service
    that a person can come to know.
The first is called *Qatnut*, "the lesser service."
In this state you may know
    that there are many heavens encircling you,
    that the earth on which you stand is
    but a tiny point,
    and that all the world is nothing
    before the Endless God—
    but even knowing all these things,
    you yourself cannot ascend.
This is still the "lesser" service.
It is of this state the prophet says:
    "from afar God appears to me."

But he who serves in *Gadlut*, "the greater service,"
    takes hold of himself with all his strength
    and his mind soars upward,
    breaking through the heavens all at once,
    rising higher,
    higher than the angels.

There are times when you are praying
  in an ordinary state of mind
  and you feel that you cannot draw near to God.
But then in an instant
  the light of your soul will be kindled
  and you will go up to the highest worlds.

You are like one who has been given a ladder:
The light that shines in you is a gift from above.

PRAYER
FOR THE
SAKE OF HEAVEN

All of man's prayers should be
for the sake of the Presence,
who herself is called prayer.
Each of man's needs is only a reflection
of some lack in the Presence.
He should pray for her fulfillment,
not merely his own.
As man brings oneness to the upper worlds
and restores that which is lacking above,
his own needs too will be fulfilled.

All the wonders that the Master performed—
healing the sick and dying,
opening the eyes of the blind,
restoring the wellsprings gone dry,
helping the barren to conceive,
great miracles that the world had not seen
since the days of Hanina ben Dosa—
All this came about because our Master thought
only of that which was lacking above.

"There is no place without Him"—
every deed man does is a dwelling-place for
God.

Maimonides says in his credo:
>   "One should pray to Him alone;
>   to no one else should he pray."

But the text can also be read:
>   "One should pray *for* Him alone;
>   for nothing else should he pray."

The purpose of Creation is only that we pray for
   God.

Material things, this world—
>   such nonsense is not worthy of prayer.

The Psalmist says:
    "A prayer of a poor man"—
But the text may also read:
    "A prayer *to* a poor man!"

Though the treasure houses of the king are full,
    they are managed by the king's officials.
Having nothing to do with all his treasures,
    the king himself is like a poor man.

He who comes in search of treasure
    will never see the King.
Only one who seeks no riches,
    who prays as to a poor man,
        can come before the King Himself.

"Do not be like those who serve the master
    in order to receive a reward.
    Be rather like those who serve the master
    not in order to receive a reward."
But another version of this text reads:
    " . . . serve the master
    in order *not* to receive a reward!"
Both versions are correct, but the latter
    speaks of a higher rung of service.

The first version surely speaks
    of a proper kind of prayer,
    one in which the worshiper
    directs his thoughts only
    to the needs of God.
It matters little to him
    whether his own personal petition
    is granted or denied.
All of this servant's deeds
    are for the sake of heaven.

But there is yet a higher rung,
    of which the second version speaks.
There is a man who lives with a burning desire
    to speak with the king.
The king has issued a decree that anyone
    who comes forward with a petition
    shall have his wish granted.
This man, however, longs only
    to stand before the king
    and speak with him always.
In him the king's decree arouses only fear:

whatever he asks, the king will grant,
and no longer will he be able to speak with him!
He would rather his petition not be granted,
so that he might have reason always
to return to the presence of the king.
This man serves ''in order
not to receive a reward.''

This is the meaning of:
''a prayer of a poor man who is faint,
pouring forth his words before the Lord.''
This poor man seeks nothing more in prayer
than that his words pour forth before the Lord.

The liturgy prescribes that
    the Prayer of Love must be recited
    before the Proclamation of God's Oneness.
The Master was told that the Messiah has not come
    because people do not
    devote themselves sufficiently to this prayer.
These words of love are the kisses
    that precede sexual union,
    awakening desire in the Presence
    so that her child, compassion,
    might come forth.

Do not rush through your weekday prayers thinking:
    "on the Sabbath I will pray with spirit."
In such prayer you would be like the king's servant
    who seems deeply attached to his tasks
    only as long as the king
    stands before him, but loses his devotion
    when the king is not in view.
This is not a faithful servant.

He who truly wants to serve will know in faith
    that there is no good
    for him in life without the King.
He will always serve as he does
    when the King stands before him.

To those beset by suffering,
  the following has been told:

There was a man who had a young child.
At times the father sought to frighten the boy.
He would dress up in strange clothing
  so that his son would not know him.
At first the child was frightened,
  but as time passed he came to know
  that this too was his father.
Then he would call out "Father!"
  and the father, filled with compassion,
  would take off the disguise
  and reveal himself to his son.

So it is with those who suffer.
When they come to understand
  that it is God Himself
  who is the source of their pain,
  they can then begin to call out to Him.
But those who do not see that all is from God
  and seek their cure elsewhere—
  these will never find true healing.

IN HIS PRESENCE

"Pour out your heart like water
in the Presence of the Lord."

On the second day of Creation,
God separated the upper and lower waters.
At the moment of their separation, we are told,
the lower waters cried out:
"We too long to be near our Creator!"

So it is with the soul:
it too once dwelt in the upper realms,
near to God,
and has fallen to the lowest depths.
Like the lower waters of Creation,
it cries out to return to God.
"Pour out your heart like the waters,"
says the Psalmist,
longing again to be
"in the Presence of the Lord."

We are told that God's name as it is spoken means
    that He is Lord of all.
But the Name as written is that of God beyond:
    He who was and is and will be,
    the source of life for all the worlds.
The very letters of this Name are themselves
    the source of life.

When a person of understanding heart begins to pray
    and comes upon the Name,
    he sees all this before him.
Can there be a greater joy than speaking face to face
    with the Eternal King, the life of every soul?
Of such moments scripture says:
    "Let Him kiss me with the kisses of His
    mouth."

Prayer is union with the Divine Presence.
Just as two people will move their bodies
    back and forth as they begin the act of love,
    so must a person accompany
    the beginning of his prayer
    with the rhythmic swaying of his body.
But as he reaches the heights of union
    with the Presence,
    the movement of his body ceases.

Be joyful always.
Know that God's Presence is with you,
    that you are looking directly at your Creator
    and your Creator at you.
Know that the Creator can do all that He desires:
    that in an instant
    He could destroy all the worlds,
    and in an instant renew them.
In Him are rooted all powers, both good and
    harmful;
His flowing life is everywhere.
Only Him do I trust!
Only Him do I fear!

What is *devequt*, or attachment to God,
    of which the masters speak?

Some say that it is a holding fast to each word—
    man's attachment to each word is so great
    that he cannot bear to part with it.

But others say that this attachment comes to one
    who truly fulfills God's commands—
    he makes his body a throne for his mind,
    his mind a throne for spirit,
    and his spirit a throne for soul.
Then his soul too becomes a throne
    for the light of the Presence
    that rests upon him.
The light spreads forth around him,
    and he, at the center of that light,
    trembles in his joy.

"When God is seated upon his throne,
    a fire of silence falls upon
    the heavenly beings."

When a person says the words of prayer
    so that they become a throne for God
    an awesome silent fire takes hold of him.
Then he knows not where he is;
    he cannot see, he cannot hear.
All this happens in the flash of an instant—
    as he ascends beyond the world of time.

It is possible to pray in such a way
      that no other person
      can know of your devotion.
Though you make no movement of your body,
      your soul is all aflame within you,
And when you cry out in the ecstasy of that
      moment—
      your cry will be a whisper.

There are times when a person's body
     may remain completely still
     while the soul serves God in silent prayer.
In such moments your prayer may be filled
     with a burning and awesome love,
     though one who sees you
     might never guess the depth
     of your inner service.
Only those who are already at one with God
     may attain this prayer
     of inner flame and outer stillness.
Such worship has greater power
     than devotion which can be seen by others.
The "shells" of evil which feed upon wayward
     prayers
     cannot reach this silent prayer,
     for it is deeply hidden within the self.

Learn to pray quietly;
>   even God's praises should be recited
>   in a low voice.
Your shouts should be whispers.
But even so, say the words with all your strength,
>   as it is written:
>   "All my bones shall say: 'O Lord, who is like
>   You!'"
Those who truly cleave to God—
>   their outcry is a whisper.

A person may come to sense two kinds of movement
    taking place within him as he prays.
At times he feels the left hand of God
    pushing him away;
        at other times God's right hand draws him near.
But even as he is pushed away,
    he still should know
    that this is only for the sake of his return.
Even as he feels
    the might of God's left hand upon him,
    he should see
    that it is God Himself who touches him.
This too he should accept in love,
    and, trembling, kiss the hand that pushes him—
    for in that very moment,
        the right hand awaits his coming near.

THOUGHTS
THAT LEAD
ASTRAY

Even the distracting thoughts
    that confound you during prayer
    may be a good sign.

In a palace surrounded by many walls
    there lives a king.
At each entrance there is a guard posted,
    to keep people from approaching.
If the petitioner who comes to see the king
    is a man of no importance,
    the guards will not bother with him.
They will allow him to enter the palace undisturbed.
In any case they know
    that the king will pay him no attention.
But how different it is
    when a respected noble of the kingdom
    tries to come before the king,
    one with a request that could endanger
    the position of the guards themselves.
Then they try to put him off
    in whatever way they can,
    telling him to leave and come back some other
    time.
How they try to keep him from the king—
    for surely his words would be accepted
    by their master!

All this is said of prayer.
When you realize that
    you are being kept away from the king,
    gather up all your strength
    and cry out in anguish:
    "Father, save me!"
God longs to hear His people's prayer—
    one cry can open all the gates.

This parable is told of prayer:

Once there was a road
    that was known to be very dangerous,
    for it passed through a forest that was filled
    with highwaymen and robbers.
These thieves would lie in wait
    for a traveller to come through the forest.
As he passed near them,
    they would pour out of their hideouts
    and fly at the throat of their victim,
    to rob for profit or simply to destroy.
Those who travelled this road were known
    to pass quickly through the forest,
    hoping to give the thieves
    no chance to fall upon them.

It happened that two men
    came to travel the way together.
One of them was very drunk, while the other was
    sober.
As they walked through the forest,
    the sober man pressed forward quickly
    until he had passed through the wood unharmed.
His drunken friend, however, lumbered slowly
    along,
    step after heavy step.
The murderers attacked him,
    beating him and covering his body
    with wounds and bruises.
But because of his drunkenness,
    he felt nothing at all.

At the far edge of the forest the two men met.
The sober man was shocked at his friend's condition

and asked him how he had managed
to survive the attack.
The drunk was no less shocked
at his companion's questions,
for he believed nothing had happened to him at
all.
Finally his friend brought him a looking-glass,
and showed him how battered and bruised he
was,
and the bloodstains that covered his clothes.
All this baffled the drunk;
He remembered nothing at all.

When a distracting thought comes to you in prayer,
　　hold fast to God and break through
　　to redeem the sacred spark
　　that dwells within that thought.

The son of a rich man was once taken captive
　　and held for ransom.
The father did nothing for his son,
　　but merely sat at home, counting out his
　　fortune.
Suddenly he saw his son before him;
The boy cried out:
　　"Father! What are you doing?
　　You have all this money—
　　stop counting and redeem your son!"

"If I am not for myself, who is for me?
     If I am only for myself, what am I?"

A person at prayer should go beyond his own self,
       no longer feeling any attachment
       to the material world.
As long as I "*am* for myself,"
       I cannot go beyond distraction.
Only when I no longer know my own existence
       will I be freed from all such thoughts.
When I have reached that rung of prayer,
       "who *is* for me?"—
       if I am no longer aware of my own self,
       what distracting thought can disturb me?

"If I am only for myself"–
       if I do think of myself
       as existing in this world,
       then I am indeed nothing.
In that case, *"what am I?"*—
       what am I worth and of what value is my
       service?
Distracting thoughts will so confound me
       that I will be as nothing,
       unable to stand before Him.

And what is man's existence but the service of God?

"No man shall go up with you;
No man shall be seen upon that mountain."

As you stand before God in prayer,
    you should feel that you stand alone—
    in all the world only you and God exist.
Then there can be no distractions;
Nothing can disturb such prayer.

Do not laugh at one who moves his body,
    even violently, during prayer.
If a man is drowning in a river,
    he makes all kinds of motions
    to try to save himself.
This is not a time for others to laugh.

Prayer is never repeated:
    the quality of each day's prayer
    is unlike that of any other.
This is the inner meaning of the Mishnah's words:
    "He whose prayer is rigid
    prays without supplication."
This can be seen even in the thoughts
    that distract us from true prayer;
They too are different every day.
Each day and its prayer,
    each day and its distractions—
    until Messiah comes.

THE WAY
OF THE
SIMPLE

The tale is told of a king who one day discovered
    that the great seal of his kingdom was missing.
You cannot imagine
    how terrible was this loss for him,
    for whoever found the seal could issue decrees
    in the king's own name.
And even if no one ever did find it,
    what a disgrace
    that the king's great seal should be
    lying in the dust!
The king was saddened by his loss,
    and his sorrow was felt
    by all the royal household.
All joined in the search—
    but because they sought so carefully
    and longed so greatly to find the seal,
    they passed it by.
Then a poor farmer happened along and,
    simply glancing about,
    he came upon the seal.
Though he knew nothing of the importance of his
    find,
    this simple farmer brought the king great joy.
The farmer also rejoiced,
    still understanding little of what he had done,
    but saying to himself:
    "The king's own seal! The king's own seal!"

The parable is not explained.

Through everything you see,
    become aware of the divine.
If you encounter love, remember the love of God.
If you experience fear, think of the fear of God.
And even in the bathroom, you should think—
    "here I am separating bad from good,
    and the good will remain for His service!"

One who reads the words of prayer with great
        devotion
            may come to see the lights within the letters,
            even though he does not understand
            the meaning of the words he speaks.
Such prayer has great power;
His mistakes in reading are of no importance.

A father has a young child whom he greatly loves.
Even though the child has hardly learned to speak,
        his father takes pleasure
        in listening to his words.

A parable is told of a man who wants to eat
    and who feels a great hunger
    for a certain food.
He then sees the very food he wants
    in a place high above him,
    beyond his reach.
In his hunger he begins to imagine
    that he is eating the food
    that he desires.
But what has he gained by such imaginings?
He is only more hungry than before.

The same is true of those who try to reach
    for the highest esoteric meaning of each prayer.
They are far from such things;
    their minds simply cannot reach
    the heights for which they strive.
What good does it do them?

Better not to reach for things beyond your grasp.

The mystics have discovered many levels of meaning
in each word of prayer.
No one person can know them all.
One who tries to meditate
on the hidden meanings of his prayer
can only reach those secrets which are known to
him.

But if in prayer a person joins
his whole self to every word,
all the secret meanings
enter the word of their own accord.
Every letter becomes a complete world.
What a great thing he does!
Worlds above are awakened by his prayer.
Thus should your prayer be fire—
for every letter awakens worlds above.

To one who moved his body violently in prayer,
    it was told:

A candle wick may be made of cotton or of flax.
With one sort of wick
    the candle makes a great deal of noise
    as it burns,
    while the other sort of candle burns in silence.
Does the silent candle give less light?

The slightest movement of your little toe,
    if it is done in truth,
    may be sufficient.

Sometimes a person at prayer feels
    that he cannot enter
    the upper world at all.
His mind remains below and he thinks:
    "The whole *earth* is full of His glory."
But really he is nearer to God than he knows.
At such times he is like a child
    who has just begun to understand
    how close to God he is.
Even though his mind cannot yet transcend this
    world,
    God is with him in his prayer.

How does so lowly a creature as man
    dare to come before God
    three times each day
    to seek fulfillment of his needs?

There was a king who had a garden
    in which he took great pride.
He hired a certain man to care for it:
    to plant, to trim, to cultivate the earth.
Now that gardener needed sustenance for himself
    and various supplies to tend the royal garden.
Should he be ashamed to come before the king
    each day and seek that which he needs?
It is for the king himself that he is working!

But such is not the case for a lazy worker,
    one who does nothing for the garden,
    but only takes what is given him
    to satisfy his gluttonous desires.
How can he dare to come again before the king and
    say:
      "Give me what I want"?

How does man have the audacity
    to ask for God's compassion?
It is only because God's love for him is like
    the love of a father for his child.
Even if the child pulls at his beard,
    a father's love is not diminished.

A parable of prayer:

A father and his son, travelling together in a wagon,
    came to the edge of a forest.
Some bushes, thick with berries,
    caught the child's eye.
"Father," he asked, "may we stop awhile
    so that I can pick some berries?"
The father was anxious to complete his journey,
    but he did not have it in his heart
    to refuse the boy's request.
The wagon was called to a halt,
    and the son alighted to pick the berries.

After a while,
    the father wanted to continue on his way.
But his son had become so engrossed in
    berry-picking
    that he could not bring himself
    to leave the forest.
"Son!" cried the father, "we cannot stay here all
    day!
    We must continue our journey!"

Even his father's pleas were not enough
    to lure the boy away.
What could the father do?
Surely he loved his son no less
    for acting so childishly.
He would not think of leaving him behind—
    but he really did have to get going
    on his journey.

Finally he called out:
    "You may pick your berries for a while longer,

but be sure that you are still able to find me,
   for I shall start moving slowly along the road.
As you work, call out 'Father! Father!'
   every few minutes, and I shall answer you.
As long as you can hear my voice,
   know that I am still nearby.
But as soon as you can no longer hear my answer,
   know that you are lost,
     and run with all your strength to find me!''

AFTER
THE HOUR
OF
PRAYER

A person at prayer is like a bed of coals,
As long as a single spark remains,
    a great fire can again be kindled.
But without that spark there can be no fire.

Always remain attached to God,
    even in those times
    when you feel unable to ascend to Him.
You must preserve that single spark—
    lest the fire of your soul be extinguished.

Take special care of what you do in the moments
    immediately after prayer.
The spirit of your worship may remain with you
    and affect your thoughts and deeds.
One who prayed with great fear of heaven
    may see his awe turn to anger.
One whose prayer was an outpouring of love
    may find himself overwhelmed by unwanted
    passion.
In order to avoid such pitfalls,
    it is best after prayer
    to begin at once your work or study.

These words require careful thought,
    but their implications are best
    not committed to writing.

The hour of formal prayer is not the only time
    when a person may seek to bind himself to God.
He who does so outside the hour of prayer,
    however,
    should take special care
    that no one else be near him
    as he ascends to the higher worlds.
Even the chirping of birds could disturb him;
Even the unspoken thought of another person
    could bring him back to earth.

When a person seeks to be alone with God,
    he should have at least one companion with
    him.
Alone one is in danger.
When two are in the same room,
    each of them may turn to God separately.
One who is more experienced
    may sometimes meditate alone in a room—
    But surely someone else should be
    in the same house with him.

There are times when you are not at prayer,
    but nevertheless you can feel close to God.
Your mind can ascend even above the heavens.

And there are also times,
    in the very midst of prayer,
    when you find yourself unable to ascend.
At such times stand where you are
    and serve with love.

A
FINAL
PARABLE

This parable is told:

There was once a musician,
    well-known for the great beauty
    of his music, who came to play before the king.
One particular melody was so loved by the king
    that he ordered the musician
    to play it for him several times each day.
And so it was.
After a time, however,
    the musician began to weary of the tune;
    no longer could he play it with the same passion
    and excitement as before.

The king, to rekindle his musician's love
    for this favorite tune,
    ordered that a man be brought in from the
    market,
    one who had never heard the tune before.
Seeing someone who had never heard him play,
    the musician's vigor was renewed,
    and he played the tune in all its beauty,
Thus the king ordered a new man brought each day.

After some time, the king sought other counsel,
    for to find a new audience each day
    was not an easy matter.
It was decided that the musician should be blinded,
    so that he never see a human form again.
Now the blind musician sat before the king,
    and whenever the king sought
    to hear his favorite tune
    he would simply say:
    "Here comes someone new,
    one who has never heard you play before!"

And the musician would play his tune
   with the greatest joy.

The parable is not explained.

NOTES

The number preceding each of the following notes refers to the page number within this book.

Citations in these notes are in accord with Hebrew works listed. Numbers refer to folio side and column in accord with pagination of traditional Hebrew works.

20 Liqqutim Yeqarim 2b.

21 Maggid Devaraw Le-Ya'aqov 27a.

22 Or Ha-Me'ir 5:31c. This translation is a free rendition, hoping to recapture the spirit of this dialogue. For a more literal translation and discussion of the passage, cf. Scholem's *The Messianic Idea in Judaism*, p. 242.

23 Toledot Ya'aqov Yosef 172c.

24 Tif'eret 'Uzi'el 134. Based on a parable attributed to Rabbi Akiba in Jerusalem Talmud Ta'anit 3:4.

25 Or Ha-Ḥokhmah 4:31b-32a.

28 Degel Maḥaneh Ephraim 234-5. The two quotations are from the daily liturgy and from Psalm 71:9.

29 Liqqutim Yeqarim 12a; Keter Shem Tov 37a.

30 Ẓawa'at RIVaSH 3a. Kabbalists placed great emphasis upon the sacred quality of the hours of dawn and dusk as proper times for prayer. Cf. Magen Avraham to Shulḥan 'Arukh, Oraḥ Ḥayyim 1:1. According to the Zohar (1:178a), the central *'Amidah* prayer, which on weekdays contains a series of petitions, should be recited immediately *after* the rising of the sun, as the moments

preceding sunrise are too intimate to be interrupted by mere petition.

31 Hit'orerut Ha-Tefillah 3a-b. The quotation is from Ecclesiastes 5:1.

32 Ẓawa'at RIVaSH 13a.

33 Ẓawa'at RIVaSH 4b-5a, 6b-7a; Liqqutim Yeqarim 1a; Siftey Ẓaddiqim 29c. The present translation is a conflate of these several versions.

34 Toledot Ya'aqov Yosef 83a.

35 Ẓawa'at RIVaSH 4a-b. There are times, however, when the masters recommend that the worshiper rush quickly through the words of prayer—perhaps so that distractions will have no chance to grab hold. Cf. p. 91 below.

36 Hit'orerut Ha-Tefillah 7b.

37 Pitgamin Qaddishin 17a. While the importance of music in Hasidism is well-known, and the wordless *niggun* became a characteristic Hasidic form of contemplation, the masters opposed the conversion of the liturgy into a platform for the ''artistic'' cantor.

40 A series of interpretations of Genesis 6:14ff., based on the dual meaning of the word *tevah*, the Biblical term for ''ark'', which can also mean ''word'' in Rabbinic Hebrew.

Or Ha-Me'ir 2:11b.

Toledot Yiẓḥaq 3a.

Ẓawa'at RIVaSH 8b. Another version in Degel Maḥaneh Ephraim 9b.

Ẓawa'at RIVaSH 8b; Ḥesed Le-Avraham 53a.

41 Shemu'ah Tovah 73b. The phrase ''the great, the pow-

erful, and the awesome'' is found in the first blessing of the daily *'Amidah* prayer, derived in turn from Deut. 10:17. According to the Kabbalists, each of these adjectives represents a particular aspect of the Divine Self: "the great" is divine love (*ḥesed*), "the powerful" is divine judgement (*din*), and "the awesome" is divine majesty (*tif'eret*) which mediates between the two others.

42 Zawa'at RIVaSH 13a.

43 Darkhey Zedeq 6b, no. 39. The creation of the universe by means of the letters of the Hebrew alphabet is a well-known motif in Jewish literature.

44 Keter Shem Tov 72b.

45 Liqqutim Yeqarim 2a; Zawa'at RIVaSH 4b.

46 Keter Shem Tov 47b, quoting Psalm 97:11.

47 Or Ha-Emet 36b. This is the heart of mystical union as portrayed in Hasidism: the soul of man is itself a part of God, cut off from its source by the veil (or illusion, to some schools) of separate existence. In prayer and contemplation, that of God which dwells within the soul, "your" God in this passage, is united with God beyond. The passage from Deut. 10:12 is taken as though it read: "with the Lord—*your* God".

48 Liqqutim Yeqarim 12a. Based on the re-reading of Psalm 150:6 found in Midrash Bereshit Rabbah 14:9 (ed. Theodor p. 134).

49 Liqqutim Yeqarim 10a; Or Torah 58b-59a.

50 Maggid Devaraw Le-Ya'aqov 17a.

51 Or Ha-Me'ir 3:16c.

54 Torey Zahav 5:4. Cf. the note to p. 40 above.

55 Or Ha-Emet 2b.

56 Maggid Devaraw Le-Ya'aqov 69a. The term "World of Thought" is a common Hasidic designation for the deepest and most hidden of the divine manifestations (*Sefirot*). The "World of Thought" comes to be revealed in the "World of Speech", the lowest of the ten manifestations, also called *Shekhinah* ("Presence"), in a way parallel to the revelation of a person's deepest thoughts in the words he speaks. The upper Sefirotic realm, that of *Ḥokhmah* or Thought, is one of complete unity, where distinctions of both individual identity and moral judgement have not yet come to be.

57 Shemu'ah Tovah 79b-80a.

58 Maggid Devaraw Le-Ya'aqov 69a. "Endless" here is used to translate *Eyn Sof*, the Kabbalistic term for the hidden Godhead. It literally means "without end".

59 'Avodat Yisra'el 98b. The author explains that one's ability to go on with reciting the liturgy at such moments surely must be a divine gift.

60 Shemu'ah Tovah 80a. The comment is on the thrice-daily recitation of Psalm 51:17 as an introduction to the *'Amidah* prayer. The Hebrew word *safah* may mean either "lip" or "riverbank". See also the following text.

61 Maggid Davaraw Le-Ya'aqov 14a.

62 Zawa'at RIVaSH 4b; Keter Shem Tov 38b. The latter source describes such a devotee as one "drunk" with prayer. The Zawa'at RIVaSH version, used in this translation, deletes the word *shikor*. Hasidim, who were accused by their enemies of excessive drinking, may have chosen to censor such a positive reference to spiritual inebriation in their early literature.

63 Maggid Devaraw Le-Ya'aqov 68b. The ram's horn (*shofar*) is used in Jewish liturgy, especially on the New Year, recalling the ram who replaced Isaac on the altar.

64 Zawa'at RIVaSH 18a. The respective values placed on the two prayer states should not be oversimplified: while *gadlut* is generally taken to be the ideal state for worship, statements in praise of the simple devotion of *qatnut* are by no means lacking in Hasidic literature. Cf. below, p. 106 and p. 115.

65 Liqqutim Yeqarim 3d.

68 Hekhal Berakhah 4:82a. "Prayer" as a name for the Shekhinah is found in earlier mystical literature. Cf. Cordovero, *Pardes Rimmonim* (ed. Munkacs) v.2, p. 45. Hanina ben Dosa was a great wonderworker and master of prayer in the first century.

69 Sefer Ba'al Shem Tov, parashat Noah, n.118. Quoted in the name of Aaron of Kaidanow, presumably by oral tradition.

70 Toledot Ya'aqov Yosef 169b. A comment on Psalm 102:1. It is made obvious in the context that neither the king nor his beloved servant will want for lack of treasures—but such treasures are not a worthy object of prayer.

71 Degel Mahaneh Ephraim 253. The passage is a comment on the saying of Antigonus of Sokho in Avot 1:3. On the two versions in that source cf. the commentary of R. Jonah Gerondi ad loc.

73 Toledot Ya'aqov Yosef 38d. The reference is to the prayer *ahavat 'olam* ("Eternal Love") which immediately precedes the recitation of the *shema'*, the proclamation of God's unity which is the center of Jewish worship.

74 Zawa'at RIVaSH 10a,

75 Orah Le-Hayyim 386b. Hasidic teachings claim that everything, including suffering and evil, comes from

God. While on one level this recognition is the basis for even the beginning of a prayer-life, final acceptance of it can be seen only as prayer's most ultimate goal.

78 Hit'orerut Ha-Tefillah 4a. Based on a Midrashic source; cf. Jellinek's *Bet ha-Midrash* 1:63 (*Midrash 'Aseret ha-Dibrot*).

79 Ketonet Passim 43b. Based on an explanation of *Tur Orah Hayyim* 5 which discusses the difference in meaning between the ineffable name YHWH and the reading *adonai*, by which the name is pronounced in the liturgy.

80 Zawa'at RIVaSH 7b. The sexual metaphor is often applied to prayer in early Hasidic literature. The passage in Toledot Ya'aqov Yosef 88c, in which the Ba'al Shem Tov is said to have called the daily *'Amidah* "the true embrace and coupling" is a paraphrase of such earlier sources as Zohar 2:128b, but with an important difference. To the earlier mystics, the coupling was envisioned as taking place *within* God; in the Hasidic reading, it is God and the worshiper who are locked in the embrace of intimacy.

81 Zawa'at RIVaSH 18a.

82 Keter Shem Tov 33a. The term *devequt* is central to Hasidic thought, particularly in the school of Dov Baer of Miedzyrzec, and is given many definitions in Hasidic literature. For a discussion of this term and its implications, cf. G. Scholem's essay "Devekuth or Communion with God" in *The Messianic Idea in Judaism*, pp. 203ff.

83 Or Ha-Emet 2b. The quotation is from the literature of Merkavah mysticism.

84 Liqqutim Yeqarim 15d.

85 Zawa'at RIVaSH 13a; Keter Shem Tov 39b-40a. The forces of evil are commonly described in Kabbalistic

sources as *qelipot* ("shells") which seek to hide the light of divinity from the world.

86 Ẓawa'at RIVaSH 4b. The quotation is from Psalm 35:10.

87 Ketonet Passim 43b. The right hand of God is traditionally associated with divine love, while the left signifies divine might and rigor.

90 Sefat Emet (by Meshulam Feibush of Brezhan), wa-era. Quoted in Sefer Ba'al Shem Tov, Noaḥ #105.

91 Divrey Mosheh 35b. The parable, attributed by the Ba'al Shem Tov to his brother-in-law R. Gershon Kitover, seems to recommend rapid prayer, so that distractions will not have a chance to enter the worshiper's mind. A shorter version of the same parable is used to prove a rather different point in Toledot Ya'aqov Yosef 194c.

93 Liqqutim Yeqarim 15c.

94 Liqqutim Yeqarim 3a; Or Torah 160b. The passage is a comment on Hillel's dictum in Avot 1:14, offering a strikingly radical re-reading of the original passage.

95 Ben Porat Yosef 88d. A comment on Exodus 34:3.

96 Liqqutim Yeqarim 15a; Keter Shem Tov 37b; Or Ha-Emet 83b.

97 Toledot Ya'aqov Yosef 67d. The quotation is from Mishnah Berakhot 4:4, here interpreted to mean that one should make the fixed prayer sufficiently flexible to allow for the special qualities of each day.

100 Liqqutim Yeqarim 3b. Truth, according to the rabbis, is God's royal seal.

101 Ẓawa'at RIVaSH 3b. The Cracow and other later editions read *bet ha-kenesset* ("synagogue") instead of *bet*

ha-kise' ("bathroom"), obviously a printer's error based on a confusion of abbreviations!

102   Liqqutim Yeqarim 2a.

103   Or Ha-Me'ir 1:10a. On early Hasidic attitudes toward esoteric prayer, cf. J. Weiss' article "The Kavvanoth of Prayer in Early Hasidism" in *Journal of Jewish Studies* 9 (1958). This text is discussed on pp. 179ff.

104   Zawa'at RIVaSH 14b; Liqqutim Yeqarim 17d. This text too is discussed in the article mentioned in the preceding note, p. 178.

105   Buzina Di-Nehora 54.

106   Zawa'at RIVaSH 7b.

107   Dibrat Shelomo 2:50b-51a. The reference is to the three prayers of the daily liturgy. The image of man as the King's gardener is well-known in Midrashic literature, based on an understanding of Genesis 2:15.

108   Kitvey Qodesh 9b.

109   Divrey Shemu'el 124. Another version of this parable is quoted by S. Y. Agnon in his *Atem Re'item*, p. 70.

112   Liqqutim Yeqarim 15b; Keter Shem Tov 37b-38a.

113   Degel Mahaneh Ephraim 131b. The passage reflects a deep and frightening awareness of the closeness between devotional states and other aspects of man's emotional life.

114   Keter Shem Tov 37b; Liqqutim Yeqarim 15b; Zawa'at RIVaSH 7b. Here the sources reflect two seemingly contradictory counsels. Could the latter be a warning against the dangers of the former?

115   Zawa'at RIVaSH 17b.

118 Or Ha-Me'ir 5:42b-c. The parable is quoted in the name of the Ba'al Shem Tov. The author of the Or Ha-Me'ir offers the suggestion that man must be blind to this world in order to see the other—an explanation which seems to escape rather than confront the frightening reality of this parable.

EDITIONS OF HASIDIC
WORKS QUOTED

'Avodat Yisra'el	Jerusalem, 1955
Ben Porat Yosef	Piotrkow, 1883
Buẓina Di-Nehora	Lvov, 1884
Darkhey Ẓedeq	Warsaw, 1877
Degel Maḥaneh Ephraim	Jerusalem, 1963
Dibrat Shelomo	Jerusalem, 1955
Divrey Mosheh	Israel, 196-? (Zolkiew)
Divrey Shemu'el	Jerusalem, 195-?
Hekhal Berakhah	Lvov, 1864
Ḥesed le-Avraham	Jerusalem, 1954
Hit'orerut Ha-Tefillah	Piotrkow, 1911
Keter Shem Tov	Beney Beraq, 1957
Ketonet Passim	New York, 1950
Kitvey Qodesh	Lvov, 1862
Liqqutim Yeqarim	Lvov, 1863
Maggid Devaraw Le-Ya'aqov	Jerusalem, 1954
Or Ha-Emet	Brooklyn, 1960
Or Ha-Ḥokhmah	Jerusalem, 1970
Or Ha-Me'ir	Israel, 1968 (Warsaw)
Or Torah	Jerusalem, 1968
Oraḥ Le-Ḥayyim	Jerusalem, 1960
Pitgamin Qaddishin	Warsaw, 1886
Sefer Ba'al Shem Tov	Szinervaraljan, 1943-Landsberg, 1948
Shemu'ah Tovah	Warsaw, 1938
Tif'eret 'Uzi'el	Tel Aviv, 1962
Toledot Ya'aqov Yosef	Jerusalem, 1966 (Korzec)
Toledot Yiẓḥaq	Warsaw, 1868
Torey Zahav	Mogilev, 1816
Ẓawa'at RIVaSH	Cracow, 1896

SUGGESTIONS FOR
FURTHER READING

Anyone with a personal or devotional interest in Hasidism should be familiar with the many works of Martin Buber on this subject. Perhaps most valuable are his *Hasidism and Modern Man* and his two volumes of *Tales of the Hasidim*, both of which are readily available in paperback editions.

The subject of prayer in Hasidism has been treated extensively by Louis Jacobs in his volume *Hasidic Prayer*, available through Schocken Press. More thorough scholarly treatments of the sources may be found in several essays by the late Joseph Weiss, published in various issues of the *Journal of Jewish Studies* (London) and in a study by Rivka Schatz entitled "Contemplative Prayer in Hasidism", published in *Studies in Mysticism and Religion Presented to G. G. Scholem*, Jerusalem, 1967.

The Hebrew reader who wants to encounter the texts in the original would do best to turn first to the section entitled *'Amud Ha-Tefillah* in S. M. Vednik's collection *Sefer Ba'al Shem Tov*, which is available in a recent reprint.